W9-DIG-523

Scotland's Glory

1. *Eilean Donan Castle, Highland Region.*

Jarrold Colour Publications, Norwich

Introduction

The name of Scotland always tends to conjure up images of a land of brooding mountain peaks, often capped with snow; vast tracts of heather-clad moorlands inhabited only by the native wildlife; storm-tossed coastlines and placid but enchanting lochs. In fact, this is the scenery which can be found in many parts of the Highlands, but Scotland is actually divided into two sections – the Highlands and the Lowlands – and it is the Lowlands that make up the largest part of the country.

There is a noticeable difference between these two sections, not only in terms of the scenery, which is much less dramatic though no less beautiful in the Lowlands, but also in their ways of life. The Highlands are sparsely populated (although the North Sea oil fields may soon change this) and the ancient traditions are still upheld here. Originally the Highlands were populated by the Picts (a Celtic race) as well as the Scots, who had actually come from Ireland, bringing the Gaelic language with them. Gaelic is still spoken in some of the remoter areas.

It was in the Highlands that the clan system originated. A clan was made up from members of the same family, led by a chief who had absolute control. Each clan could be identified by the colour and design of its tartan. Unfortunately, family loyalties led to frequent feuds between clans, and indeed the whole history of the Highlands was turbulent.

The romantic Scottish hero Bonnie Prince Charlie (the Young Pretender) gathered the clans together in 1745 in an attempt to proclaim his father, James, the Old Pretender, king of Scotland, but this uprising ended in disaster when they were defeated by the English at the battle of Culloden. After this battle, the clan system was broken up by the Duke of Cumberland, victor of Culloden.

In complete contrast to the Highlands, the Lowlands are densely populated, with many bustling towns and cities offering every possible facility that a visitor could desire. The face of the Lowlands is constantly changing, as the grim Victorian tenement buildings are pulled down and replaced by modern housing. Industry is important here, and also agriculture, for the land is much more fertile than that of the Highlands.

The whole of Scotland is wrapped in an aura of romance, heightened by the fascinating and often heroic figures who lived here. Bonnie Prince Charlie was perhaps one of the most colourful characters to emerge from its history, but the tragic Mary Queen of Scots should not be forgotten, nor the Highland outlaw Rob Roy MacGregor who, like a Scottish Robin Hood, made many raids on the richer areas in the south and west of the country. He was often immortalised in ballads, and certainly Scotland has inspired many writers to preserve the country's old songs and legends in verse and in novels. Robert Burns was undoubtedly its greatest poet, his work concentrating mainly on Scottish themes, speech and traditions, and Sir Walter Scott its greatest novelist. Through their works, much of Scottish life in earlier times can be recaptured.

3. *A Highland piper with his bagpipes.*

The River Shiel, Glen Shiel, Highland Region.

Borders

The Borders Region lies in southern lowland Scotland and, as its name suggests, it marks the boundary between England and Scotland. The border line runs along the crest of the Cheviot Hills, and for some miles the great River Tweed, famous for salmon-fishing, runs along its course.

This is a region of undulating river valleys, moorlands, gentle hills and pastures cropped by sheep but the scene has not always been so tranquil here, as the ruined abbeys of Dryburgh, Jedburgh, Melrose and Kelso testify. These famous Border monasteries were all gutted many centuries ago in raids by English invaders, as their situation made them particularly vulnerable to attack. Dryburgh Abbey, beautifully situated in a loop of the Tweed, was attacked and badly damaged several times by the English, yet its cloister buildings have survived relatively unscathed. Of the church itself, however, only the west front and parts of the nave, transept and chapter-house can still be seen. Field-Marshal Earl Haig and Sir Walter Scott are buried here.

The Borders Region is devoted mainly to agriculture and sheep farming, but the wool industry is important in several towns in the Tweed valley, and Galashiels and Selkirk are noted for their tweed mills. The market town of Kelso was described by Sir Walter Scott as 'the most beautiful, if not the most romantic, village in Scotland'. The abbey here was once the greatest of the Border group of abbeys, but it was destroyed in 1545 by the Earl of Hereford and very little of its structure remains. Another interesting architectural feature of Kelso is the five-arched bridge which spans the Tweed. Built by John Rennie in 1803, this bridge was used as a model for Rennie's Waterloo Bridge (now demolished) in London.

In earlier centuries it was necessary to protect the Scottish border from English invasions with strongholds such as Hermitage Castle, dating from the fourteenth century. Its history has been turbulent, and in 1566 it was visited by Mary Queen of Scots. She had come to see her paramour, the Earl of Bothwell, who owned the castle at that time, and she rode to and from Jedburgh (a distance of some forty miles) in one day. She nearly died from a fever brought on by this journey.

A castle with an equally exciting history is Neidpath Castle, originally a Fraser stronghold but later owned by the Earls of Tweeddale. During the Civil War, the Earl held the castle for Charles I but was forced to surrender after Cromwell's artillery battered the eleven-foot-thick walls.

A relic of more peaceful times are the great houses found throughout the region. Traquair House is one of the oldest inhabited mansions in Scotland, and was once the court of William the Lion. Altogether, twenty-seven monarchs, both English and Scottish, have stayed here. Traquair was immortalised by Sir Walter Scott as 'Tully-veolan' in *Waverley*.

The Borders Region is true Sir Walter Scott country and his writing was inspired both by the romance of its scenery and also by the many local tales and legends. Here Scott lived, from 1812 until his death in 1832, at the mansion of Abbotsford, near Melrose. This was just a tiny farm until it was bought and improved by Sir Walter. The mansion was largely designed by him and since then his rooms, including a library of 20,000 books, have remained unchanged. The drawing room contains some interesting portraits, while in the armoury can be seen a comprehensive collection of historic weapons from all ages. Sir Walter also planted many of the trees on the estate.

Scott was not the only great writer to be associated with the region. The poet James Hogg, 'The Ettrick Shepherd', was born in the Vale of Ettrick and, before moving to Edinburgh, he herded sheep on the hills around the romantic St Mary's Loch. His statue stands close by, near 'Tibble Shiel's' Inn, which was a favourite haunt of his.

4. *Part of the ruins of Dryburgh A*

5. *The town of Kelso stands by the River Tweed.*

8. *St Mary's Loch overlooked by Broad La one of the highest of t Lowland hil*

6. *A house has stood on the site of Traquair House for about 1,000 years.*

9. *Hermitage Castle dramatically situated bleak moorlar*

7. *Abbotsford House seen from the banks of the River Tweed.*

10. *The fifteenth-centr Neidpath Castle wa Fraser strongho*

Central

The Central Region is particularly rewarding for it is crossed by the 'Highland Boundary Fault' – the geographical line which divides the Highlands from the Lowlands – and so exhibits scenery characteristic of both. Some of the higher Highland peaks, such as Ben More at 3,843 feet, are found in this region along with an abundance of beautiful lochs, including Loch Lubnaig which is a genuine Highland loch. However, there are also gentle, low-lying glens where agriculture is practised.

Perhaps the most spectacular scenery can be found in the gorge of the Trossachs, which stretches from Loch Achray to Loch Katrine. The name literally means 'bristly country', and the landscape is made up of lochs and rivers, surrounded by dense woodlands of oaks, hazels, birches and rowans, and overlooked by rugged mountain peaks.

Fame came to the Trossachs not only because of their undoubted beauty but also because they were described by Sir Walter Scott in his romantic poem *The Lady of the Lake*. The subsequent fame of this work attracted many visitors during the early nineteenth century. The 'Lady' of the poem was Ellen Douglas and her 'Lake' was Loch Katrine. Loch Katrine is still just as lovely, but today it is also used as a reservoir, supplying fresh water to Glasgow.

Another well-loved loch in the Trossachs is Loch Ard, noted for its forest which is part of the Queen Elizabeth Forest Park. To the east of the loch is Aberfoyle, a holiday resort known as the 'Gateway to the Trossachs'. This has associations with Sir Walter Scott's *Rob Roy*, while two nearby waterfalls are described in his *Waverley*.

Overlooking Loch Ard are the Menteith Hills and nestling at their feet is Port of Menteith, on the shore of the Lake of Menteith. This is the only natural sheet of water in Scotland to be called a 'lake'. On the largest of its three islands are the ruins of the Augustinian Inchmahome Priory, which was founded in 1238. This priory must hold many historic memories, for Robert the Bruce visited it on three occasions and Mary Queen of Scots, aged only four at the time, stayed here for a few weeks after the battle of Pinkie in 1547.

The entire Central Region is rich in traces of history. Near the resort of Killin, for example, is the island of Inch Buie which was the burial ground of the Clan MacNab, and also an ancient beheading pit, thought to be the last remaining example in Scotland. The Royal Burgh of Stirling, however, undoubtedly has the most to offer. This great town, called the 'Gateway to the Highlands', stands on a bend of the River Forth and in earlier centuries it was the last place where the Forth could be crossed before its estuary widened. Several battles were fought around the bridge here. Towering over the town, perched on top of a high rock, is the ancient Stirling Castle; scene of many skirmishes between Scots and English in the past. In 1314 Robert the Bruce fought, and won, the battle of Bannockburn for possession of the castle. Later it was to become a royal residence, vying with Edinburgh Castle. In 1651 the castle was captured by General Monk but in 1746 Prince Charles Edward failed to take it. Both James II and James V were born here, and it was James V who was responsible for the palace buildings here, turning Stirling Castle into one of the most splendid buildings of its kind in Scotland. In 1594 James VI rebuilt the Chapel Royal for the christening of Prince Henry. Today, the castle is used as a barracks.

While most of the Central Region is primarily agricultural in nature, industry is dominant in the area around Stirling. Falkirk, for example, is important for its coal mines and the great Carron ironworks, while Grangemouth, a port on the Forth estuary, is equally important as an oil refinery and a shipbuilding centre. It has the largest complex of oil installations, refineries and allied works in Scotland.

12. *The Port of Menteith is a popular reso*

11. *Loch Lubnaig lies beneath steep hills.*

13. *Stirling Castle overlooks Bannockburn battlefield.*

14. *Loch Ard is a beautiful sheet of water, surrounded by trees, in the Trossachs.*

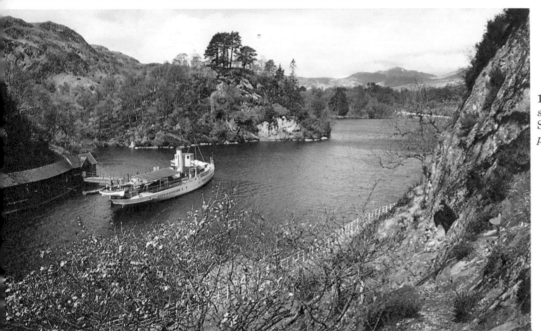

15. *The pleasure-steamer* Sir Walter Scott *moored at the pier on Loch Katrine.*

16. *The village of Tyndrum is a popular resort for climbers as it is surrounded by fine mountains.*

17. *The River Docha* *seen here at Killin,* *graced by many litt* *waterfal.*

Dumfries & Galloway

Dumfries and Galloway is the extreme south-western region of Scotland, displaying a wealth of hills, dales and upland moors as well as a long stretch of coastline. Part of the coast overlooks the sandy shores of the Solway Firth, but on the whole the coastline is rugged, with the occasional 'smugglers' cave.

There are many fishing villages and harbours scattered along this shoreline. The little resort of Portpatrick was once a packet station for steamers sailing from Northern Ireland, although this service has now been transferred to Stranraer. Kirkcudbright, on the Dee estuary, also has a little harbour although this ancient Royal Burgh has always been most important as a market town. A prominent feature here is the ruined MacLellan's Castle which was built in 1582. This stands on the site of two previous castles.

Moving inland, most of the region is covered by glacial deposits and the land is mostly used to cultivate fodder for the dairy cattle and sheep that are reared here. The most important crops are turnips, oats and rotation grasses. The most beautiful scenery is found in the dales, particularly the three parallel dales of Eskdale, Annandale and Nithsdale. Many prehistoric remains can be seen around Eskdale.

In Nithsdale is the Royal Burgh of Dumfries, situated on the banks of the River Nith. Five bridges span this river and the oldest of these was built in the fifteenth century by Lady Devorgilla. The town is wreathed in history, for it was here, in 1306, that Robert the Bruce changed the entire course of Scottish history by stabbing his rival, the 'Red Comyn'. A plaque marks the spot in Castle Street.

There are numerous relics of Robert Burns to be found throughout Dumfries, for he actually wrote many of his poems here, including 'Auld Lang Syne'. He came to live in the town in 1791, at first renting a small flat and then moving to a house in Mill Vennel, now known as Burns Street. He died in this house in 1796 and it is now a museum, containing his manuscripts. Burns and his wife, Jean Armour, along with several of their children, lie buried in the churchyard of St Michael.

Nithsdale is also the setting for Drumlanrig Castle, standing among woods just a little to the west of the river. This magnificent building was constructed in the seventeenth century for the first Duke of Queensberry. He, however, was so horrified by the expense of its construction that he could only bring himself to spend one night in it. In 1745 it was occupied by Prince Charles Edward, and today it is the home of the Duke of Buccleuch. It is surrounded by lovely parkland, in which stands the ruined Tibber's Castle, destroyed by Bruce in 1311.

Some of the wildest and most isolated scenery in Scotland can be found in the area known as the Galloway Highlands. The highest mountain here is Merrick, at 2,764 feet, and there is also a range of barren mountains known as the Rhinns of Kells. Herds of stately red deer can sometimes be glimpsed on these lonely slopes, and if you are very lucky you might spot a golden eagle soaring from the mountain top.

Beneath these lofty hills lies the narrow Loch Trool, surrounded by the vast area of the Galloway Forest Park which is about 200 square miles in extent. Conifers line the banks of the loch and the magnificent Highland scenery of the area has inspired many modern-day writers such as John Buchan, author of *The Thirty-Nine Steps*.

At the north end of the loch Robert Bruce won a victory over an English force by pelting the enemy with rocks thrown from the slopes of Mulldonach. Also in this area is a monument which commemorates a Covenanters' skirmish (the Covenanters were a Scottish religious group dedicated to keeping the Presbyterian form of worship) which took place in 1685. Throughout the seventeenth century this district was very much involved with the Covenanters' movement.

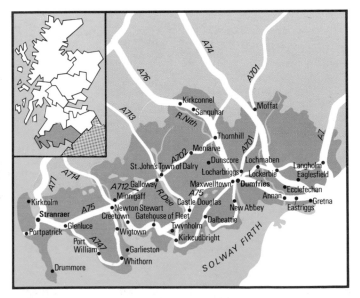

18. *Glen Trool, a haven for wi*

19. *Orchardton Tower, near Palnackie, is a unique fifteenth-century circular tower house. The village of Palnackie lies on an inlet of the Solway Firth.*

20. *Loch Trool, in the Galloway Highlands.*

21. *Sunset over the Nith estuary, near Glencaple.*

24. *Drumlanrig Castle stands amid woodland in Nithsdale.*

2. *Fishing boats moored in the little harbour at Kirkcudbright, on the Dee estuary.*

25. *The River Nith flows through the ancient Royal Burgh of Dumfries.*

26. *Lovely forests clothe the hillside around Loch Ken.*

. This bridge spans e River Esk at ntpath.

27. *The small fishing and holiday resort of Portpatrick.*

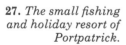

Fife

Fife lies between the great firths of Forth and Tay, which are spanned respectively by two famous railway bridges: the 2,765⅓-yard-long Forth Bridge, which was built in 1883–90 and is one of the finest examples of engineering in the world; and the Tay Bridge, which is two miles long. This was built in 1883–8, but its predecessor was destroyed in a disastrous gale, in 1879, killing many passengers in a train which was crossing at the time.

Most of the region consists of flat, fertile land which gives a high yield of wheat and oats. Along the coastline are scattered many seaside resorts and ports, several of which are Royal Burghs. One such is Pittenweem, with its ancient little harbour around which houses are grouped in attractive terraces, while the fishing town of Crail (once a haunt of smugglers) is equally picturesque.

In the old town of Culross there is a fine thirteenth-century church with a nave that is now in ruins, but undoubtedly the most important examples of religious architecture in the region are St Andrews Cathedral and Dunfermline Abbey.

For six centuries the Royal Burgh of Dunfermline was the capital of Scotland, and the town grew up around its Benedictine abbey. This abbey was founded in the eleventh century by Queen Margaret, and the remains of her original church still lie beneath the nave, which was built in late Norman times. To the east of this can be seen traces of the thirteenth-century St Margaret's shrine, still a place of pilgrimage for Scottish Catholics. The abbey is a fitting burial place for many of Scotland's kings, including King Robert I (Robert the Bruce) who was buried in the choir in 1329. His grave, in front of the altar, was only identified for certain in the early nineteenth century when his skeleton was discovered during some reconstruction work. Although his body lies in Dunfermline, his heart is interred at Melrose.

The greatest Catholic religious centre in Scotland, however, is St Andrews, once the country's ecclesiastical capital. Its importance stemmed from the tradition that the bones of St Andrew the Apostle were brought here by St Regulus. The magnificent cathedral was founded in 1161 but was not completed until 1318, by which time it was the largest church in Scotland. However, in 1559 after a series of preachings on 'The Cleansing of the Temple' by John Knox, leader of the Scottish Protestant religious reformers, much of the cathedral's beautiful ornamentation was destroyed. Gradually it fell altogether into ruin, partly from neglect and partly because many of its stones were stolen by the local population to be used for building their own houses. All that remains of it today are parts of the east and west ends, and a portion of the nave's south wall.

St Andrews also boasts the oldest university in Scotland, founded in 1412. Despite its great age, it is small in size, with only a few surviving university buildings. In 1897 University College, Dundee, was incorporated with St Andrews but has since been separated again.

Over the past centuries, then, St Andrews has been renowned both as a religious centre and as a seat of learning, yet these days it is probably best known as the 'Mecca of golfers'. Here is the almost legendary Old Course, which dates back to the fifteenth century and is the oldest golf course in the world, and here also is the Royal and Ancient Golf Club which is the world's ruling authority on the game.

Near the golf links, on a rock overlooking the sea, stand the gaunt ruins of the ancient St Andrew's Castle. This was the scene of many tragedies, including the murder of Cardinal Beaton in 1546. A historic building with happier associations is Falkland Palace in the Royal Burgh of Falkland. Built at the start of the sixteenth century on the site of an earlier castle, this palace became the favourite residence of the Scottish court. James V was responsible for many building improvements here, and his daughter, Mary Queen of Scots, enjoyed hunting from the palace.

28. *The ancient harbour at Pittenwe*

30. *St Andrews Cathedral was once Scotland's largest chur*

32. *The Mercat Cross, Culro*

29. *Crail is a beautiful fishing town.*

31. *The historic Falkland Palace.*

33. *The great Benedictine abbey of Dunfermli*

Grampian

Grampian, Scotland's most easterly region, has an extensive and varied landscape, much of which has been moulded by the action of the great River Dee which crosses the region. The Dee, famous for its salmon, is the fifth longest river in Scotland, and the upper part of its beautiful wooded valley is known as 'Royal Deeside'.

For centuries this area has been the playground of Scottish kings, who enjoyed hunting in the surrounding hills, but it was only comparatively recently that it earned the title of 'Royal'. In 1848 Queen Victoria and her consort, Prince Albert, visited the estate of Balmoral on the shores of the Dee. They were so struck by the beauty of this place that, four years later, Prince Albert purchased the estate. The original mansion house was rebuilt in the Scots baronial style and some years later the parish church of Crathie was also rebuilt. Today the Royal Family still worship at Crathie church when they are in residence at Balmoral Castle.

Many of Scotland's traditions are upheld in Royal Deeside at the Braemar Highland Gathering which takes place every September and is attended by members of the Royal Family. Here competitions in athletics and Highland dancing are the main attractions, as the glorious music of the pipers sounds in the background.

Although Balmoral Castle is the best known, there are many other baronial castles throughout the region and they are mostly still inhabited. Ballindalloch Castle dates mainly from the sixteenth century, although there are some later additions, while Crathes Castle was also built in the sixteenth century. Crathes is now owned by the National Trust for Scotland but still bears the stamp of four centuries of family life. It contains many architectural treasures, and its formal gardens are particularly beautiful. The delightful Invercauld House overlooks the River Dee, and nearby is the famous Old Brig O' Dee which was built by General Wade 200 years ago and has perfectly withstood the test of time.

The most important city in the region, and indeed the third largest in all of Scotland, is Aberdeen. This is also the largest fishing port in Scotland, lying on the estuaries of the Dee and Don. Commercially, its many industries include engineering, shipbuilding and, recently, the vitally important North Sea oil project.

The city is largely built from a glistening, pale grey granite and architecturally it is most noteworthy for its university and its cathedral. The medieval cathedral of St Machar was founded in about 1136, although the earliest surviving portion dates from the fourteenth century. This is a fortified building, with twin towers on the west front, some fine wooden nave bosses and a magnificent painted wooden nave ceiling of 1540. The cathedral choir has long since vanished.

One of the finest ecclesiastic buildings in Scotland is the ruined Elgin Cathedral, built in 1224. In its prime, the cathedral was so magnificent that it was known as the 'Lanthorn of the North', with its twin western towers soaring above the surrounding landscape. Disaster overtook it in 1390 when it was burnt by the notorious outlaw the 'Wolf of Badenoch', son of King Robert II. This act of destruction was performed in revenge for the sentence of excommunication which had been passed upon him. In the years that followed, the roof of the cathedral was stripped of its lead and in 1711 the central tower collapsed.

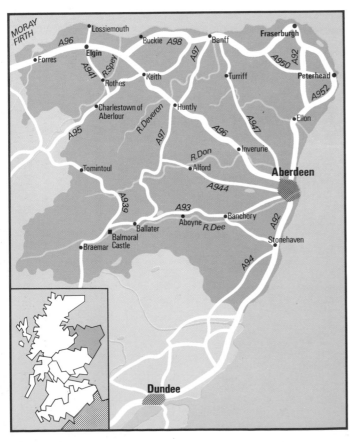

35. *The ruined Dunnottar Castle was founded in the fourteenth century. It held out against Cromwell's troops until 1652.*

36. *Balmoral Castle is the Scottish residence of the Royal Family. It stands in beautiful grounds.*

37. *Crathes Castle contains some magnificent painted ceilings which date from 1599.*

38. *Tossing the caber is one of the main events at the Braemar Highland Games.*

39. *Invercauld House is sometimes said to enjoy the best view on Deeside.*

40. *The fishing village of Portknockie has a fine natural harbour.*

42. *Ballindallo Castle is surround by beautiful groun*

43. *The Old Brig Dee spans the Ri Dee at Invercau*

41. *Aberdeen is the largest fishing port in Scotland.*

44. *Elgin Cathedr the 'Lanthorn of Nor*

Highland

The Highland Region is both the largest and most northerly of Scotland, and it is here that the truly dramatic and isolated scenery so often associated with Scotland can be found. Not all of the scenery is mountainous, however, and one of the region's most interesting natural features is in fact the rift valley of Glen More, or the Great Glen, as it is known.

The Great Glen stretches from Inverness to Fort William, dividing the mainland into two portions. Running through the glen is a chain of lochs (the largest of which is Loch Ness) which are linked together by the Caledonian Canal. This canal, with its twenty-nine locks, was the work of the famous engineer Thomas Telford. Construction began in 1803 and was only finished after forty-four years but the completion of the canal meant that small ships could travel straight across Scotland from the North Sea to the Atlantic Ocean without having to navigate round stormy Cape Wrath.

Loch Ness is probably the best known of all the Scottish lochs because of the monster which is supposed to inhabit its murky depths. The Loch Ness Monster was first sighted as far back in history as the seventh century and since then sightings have been reported many times. Its existence has not yet been proved, however.

Towering over Loch Ness and the Great Glen is a fine succession of mountains, including the flat-topped Cairngorm range which is so popular for winter sports. At the western end of the glen is the highest mountain in Britain, Ben Nevis (4,406 feet) and the magnificent valley of Glencoe. Despite its beauty, Glencoe holds tragic memories, and is sometimes called the Glen of Weeping. Here in 1692 about forty members of the Clan Macdonald were massacred by a troop of soldiers led by Campbell of Glen Lyon.

The north-west Highlands stretching beyond Glen More contain the really dramatic mountain scenery for which Scotland is so renowned. Here rugged peaks are reflected in the clear and icy waters of lochs fringed by pine trees. Herds of deer roam through the forests, birds of prey soar from the mountain tops, and the distinctive Highland cattle graze on the lonely moorlands. The coastline is barren and rugged, with miles of cliff scenery towering above the sea.

Offshore is the Isle of Skye, also romantically known as the 'Winged Isle' or the 'Isle of Mists'. It is the largest of the Inner Hebrides group, measuring some fifty miles in length, yet no part of the island is more than five miles distance from the sea. Skye is probably the loveliest of all the Scottish islands with its rocky coastline indented by sea-lochs, fine cliff scenery and fantastic rock formations. The island is dominated by the serrated peaks of the Cuillin mountains, which are often almost hidden by swirling mists which can envelope the landscape. Because of the rough surface of the rock from which they are formed, the Cuillins offer some of the finest rock climbing in the world as well as probably the most spectacular rock scenery in Great Britain.

The pace of life in the isle is unhurried and its people are renowned for their courtesy and hospitality. Their way of life has changed relatively little over the centuries and most of the islanders still make their living from crofting and fishing. Tradition is strong here and Skye is wreathed in legends and tales of the fairy folk. Its history is also inextricably bound up with the adventures of the Young Pretender, Bonnie Prince Charlie, who fled to the island after his defeat at the battle of Culloden Moor in 1746. He was aided in his escape by the Jacobite heroine Flora Macdonald, who is buried here on the island at Kilmuir.

46. *The port of Helmsdale lies between ridges of moorland.*

48. *The Glenfinnan Monument commemorates the unfurling of Bonnie Prince Charlie's banner in 1745.*

47. *Fort George is a fine artillery fortification.*

49. *Old Leanach Cottage, on the site of the battle of Culloden of 1746.*

50. *Cawdor Castle is one of Scotland's finest medieval buildings.*

51. *Duncansby Head is the north-easterly point of the Scottish mainland.*

53. *The beautiful and remote Loch Assynt.*

54. *For centuries, Dunrobin Castle was the seat of the Earls of Sutherland.*

Ben Eighe, viewed from Bridge of Crudie.

55. *Glencoe, scene of a bloody massacre in 1692.*

. *Sunset over Loch Eil.*

57. *The River Moriston, Glen Moriston.*

58. *The Cairngorm range from the Boat of Garten.*

59. *The sea-loch Shieldaig is an inlet of Loch Torridon.*

62. *Plockton lies sheltered inlet of Car*

60. *Loch Ness is supposedly the home of a monster.*

63. *Loch Oich belo to the chain of loch the Great G*

61. *Shaggy Highland cattle roam the lonely moorlands.*

64. *The historic tou Inverness lies or River*

65. *Loch Maree is overlooked by the 3,260-foot-high Ben Slioch.*

67. *Loch Torridor overlooked by r sandstone mountai.*

68. *The Comman Memorial at Spe Bridge, in memory the Second World V Commandos u trained he*

69. *The harbour Portree, capital of Isle of Sk*

66. *Loch Ewe and the beautiful gardens of Inverewe House.*

71. *Sunset over the Isle of Skye, seen from Mallaig.*

72. *Towering above Loch Linnhe is Ben Nevis.*

70. *The wild and craggy Storr on the Isle of Skye.*

*. Castle Tioram and
och Moidart are
urrounded by wild
nd mountainous
untryside.*

75. *Fort Augustus, in
the Great Glen, was
built after the 1715
rising.*

76. *Aviemore is a very
popular winter-sports
centre in the
Cairngorms.*

77. *The village of
Durness lies near the
rugged Cape Wrath.*

*Loch Broom is a
-loch. The resort of
apool stands by its
uth.*

Lothian

Lothian as a region always seems to be overshadowed by the immense fame of Edinburgh, the capital city of Scotland, which lies within its boundaries.

There is, however, much more to the region than this great city. Lothian is a fertile land, bordered to the south by the ranges of the Pentland, Moorfoot and Lammermuir hills, and to the north by the Firth of Forth. The Forth Road Bridge, which was opened by the Queen in 1964, links Lothian to the neighbouring district of Fife. Throughout the Lothian region, then, are lovely stretches of hilly countryside, coastal scenery, towns and villages, castles and palaces; all of which are well worth exploring.

Edinburgh certainly dominates the region because of its dramatic and commanding situation. Like Rome, it is built upon seven hills and it is overlooked by the 823-foot-high extinct volcano known as Arthur's Seat.

The city took over from Perth as the capital of Scotland in the fifteenth century, when James II held his parliament here, but Edinburgh is known to have existed for several centuries previously. Today it is divided into the Old Town and the New Town, lying side by side, but until about 200 years ago Edinburgh consisted only of the Old Town, clustered upon a sloping rock which is surmounted by an imposing castle.

Centuries of violent history are crammed into Edinburgh Castle, for a fortification has stood on this site for at least 1,000 years, and its earliest surviving portion is St Margaret's Chapel, dating from *c.* 1100. The castle has changed hands many times – in 1296 it was occupied by Edward I and some time later it was refortified by Edward III. In 1341 it was captured by the Scots but in 1650 it was taken by Cromwell during his occupation of Scotland. During his occupation, the ancient insignia of Scottish royalty, including the crown and sceptre, were hidden away but they were rediscovered in 1817 and are now displayed in the castle's Crown Chamber.

Stretching along the ridge of Castle Rock is the Royal Mile, which ends at the Palace of Holyroodhouse, Scotland's most important Royal Palace. Its construction was begun by James IV in 1550, but most of the existing palace was built for Charles II. For six years, from 1561 to 1567, the ill-fated Mary Queen of Scots lived in private apartments in the palace and it was here that her Italian secretary, David Rizzio, was stabbed to death in her presence by her husband, Darnley, and a group of other noblemen in March 1566.

Darnley (who was himself murdered) and Rizzio were both buried in the adjoining Holyrood Abbey. This abbey was pillaged and plundered several times and all that remains of it today is its nave and west front.

Forming a complete contrast to the steep little roads and the jumble of buildings in the Old Town is the dignified design of the late eighteenth-century New Town with its carefully laid-out broad streets and elegant squares. Many of the new buildings, such as those making up the University and Charlotte Square, were the work of the great Georgian architect Robert Adam.

The best known thoroughfare in the New Town is Princes Street, which on one side is crowded with shops and hotels. The other side opens out on to the beautiful Princes Street Gardens, with the dramatic edifice of the castle towering above them.

At about the same time that the New Town was coming into creation, Edinburgh began to blossom as a centre of culture, with such eminent men as Sir Walter Scott, Robert Burns and the philosopher David Hume numbered among its residents. These days the Edinburgh Festival is held here annually and includes among its attractions a floodlit Military Tattoo outside the castle, and performances of operas, concerts and plays. The Festival draws vast crowds of spectators.

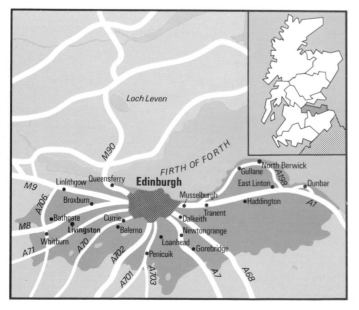

Views of Edinburgh. Above **(78):** *John Knox's house.* Below **(79):** *The Castle from the Vennel.* Top right **(80):** *The Castle and Princes Street Gardens.* Centre right **(81):** *The band of the Royal Scots Guards on the Castle Esplanade.* Bottom right **(82):** *The Palace of Holyroodhouse.*

83. *The eighteenth-century Hopetoun House is one of the most splendid mansions of its period in Scotland.*

84. *The massive remains of Dirleton Castle date mainly from the thirteenth century.*

85. *The Forth Road Bridge is one of the longest suspension bridges in Europe.*

86. *The Dugald Stewart monument seen from Calton Hill, with Edinburgh in the background.*

87. *The now-ruined Linlithgow Palace was destroyed by a fire in 1746.*

88. *Tantallon Castle was built in 1375 and overlooks the Bass Rock.*

Strathclyde

Although Edinburgh is the capital of Scotland, it is Glasgow, in the Strathclyde Region, which is actually the largest city in the country. Its size and importance is due mainly to its prime situation on the River Clyde, for over the years following the Industrial Revolution it has developed rapidly into an enormously important seaport and a centre of world commerce. Industry flourishes on Clydeside because of the proximity of local coalfields. Chief among these industries is shipbuilding (the great liners *Queen Mary* and *Queen Elizabeth* were built here) but there are also engineering and ironworks as well as such diverse industries as textile, glass and chemical manufacture.

Like Edinburgh, Glasgow has a very distinctive character, and an even longer history. Originally growing up around a fording-place on the River Clyde, it is traditionally said to have been founded by St Kentigern (also known as St Mungo) who built a church here in the sixth century. A cathedral, completed in 1136, was built on the same site but burnt down about fifty years later. It was quickly rebuilt, however, and today is the only complete medieval cathedral on the Scottish mainland.

In 1451 a university was founded by papal bull. Originally it occupied buildings in the High Street but it is now housed in an imposing Gothic structure which was designed by Sir George Gilbert Scott.

Despite the rapid growth of Glasgow's industrial complex there are many peaceful gardens and parks to be found within this otherwise bustling city, while the scenery surrounding it is often breathtaking. Just a few miles away is Loch Lomond, the 'Queen of Scottish lakes' which, at about twenty-four miles long, is the largest stretch of water in Great Britain.

Because of Glasgow's position near the coastline, it is surrounded by sea-lochs stretching their arms far inland. It is also within easy reach of the beautiful islands which make up the Inner Hebrides. One of the nearest is the Isle of Bute, separated from the mainland by the narrow stretch of water known as the Kyles of Bute. To its west, Bute is sheltered by the long, narrow peninsula of Kintyre, while beyond Kintyre lie the islands of Jura and Islay. At its southernmost end, Islay is only twenty-five miles away from Northern Ireland.

The Isle of Mull is the largest of the Inner Hebrides. Although it is only about thirty miles in length, its rugged coastline, indented by sea-lochs, actually measures 300 miles. Mull can easily be reached from the mainland by taking a steamer from the busy resort of Oban. The Oban steamers also call at several of the other islands, including Iona which, despite its tiny size, is known throughout the world for its early religious associations. Christianity was brought to Scotland from Ireland by St Columba, who landed at Iona in AD 563. Here he set up a humble monastery and after his death the island became a place of pilgrimage. The monastery was ravaged several times by raiding Norsemen, but in 1203 a new monastery was founded by the Benedictines. This was destroyed in 1561. The oldest surviving building on the island is St Oran's Chapel, built by Queen Margaret in 1080, and St Oran's Cemetery is the burial place of many ancient kings of Scotland, Ireland and even Norway. For centuries this graveyard was believed to be the nearest place to Heaven.

In the thirteenth century a cathedral was founded on Iona, though it has been greatly added to and restored so that most of the present structure is fifteenth century. It is cruciform in shape and has a low, square tower. Outside the cathedral is the granite St Martin's Cross, over sixteen feet high and carved with intricate Runic symbols.

90. *The magnificent staircase at Culzean Castle, which was designed by Robert Adam.*

92. *Loch Awe is a par[t] Scotland's most import[ant] hydroelectric sche[me]*

93. *Oban is a famous [West] Highland resort [and] yachting cen[tre]*

91. *Rothesay is the principal town on the Isle of Bute.*

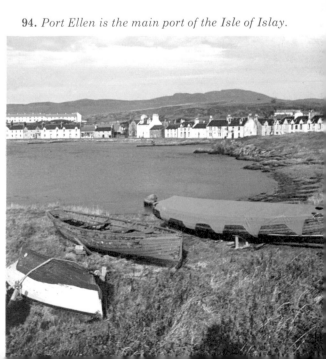

94. *Port Ellen is the main port of the Isle of Islay.*

95. *The birthplace of Robert Burns, at Alloway.*

96. *The cathedral and the ruined abbey of Iona.*

97. *Sunset over the Isle of Luing from Arduaine.*

98. *The narrow sea-loch of Loch Long.*

99. *The Art Gallery and Museum in Glasgow.*

100. *Inveraray Castle is the seat of the Duke of Argyll.*

102. *Sunset over L Na Lathaich, on Isle of M*

101. *Dunderave Castle overlooks the magnificent Loch Fyne.*

103. *The fifteenth-century Brodick Castle, Isle of Arran.*

104. *Lonely Loch Eck lies in the Cowal peninsula.*

Tayside

In the very centre of Scotland, Tayside exhibits a great range of scenery but, of course, it is the River Tay which is its most important natural feature. The Tay carries a larger volume of water than any other river in Great Britain and it is the longest of all Scottish rivers. It rises on the slopes of Ben Lui in Strathclyde and finally flows into the North Sea by Dundee, thus giving it an overall length of 117 miles.

For some fifteen miles of its course it flows through Loch Tay, which is famed for its salmon fishing. Overlooking the loch is Ben Lawers, which at 3,984 feet high is the loftiest peak in the region, while in Loch Tay are several wooded islands, one of which bears traces of an ancient priory. To the east is the village of Kenmore. Here a bridge, built in 1744, crosses the River Tay and Robert Burns so admired the view from the bridge that he wrote a poem in its praise over the fireplace of the village inn.

Of the many other fine lochs in the region, Loch Tummel is particularly lovely. The road which runs along its north shore leads to Queen's View, a famous viewpoint visited by Queen Victoria in 1866. From here can be seen the fabulous quartzite peak of Schiehallion, a 3,547-foot-high mountain. Loch Tummel forms part of the important Tummel-Garry hydro-electric scheme, and in order to implement this it was necessary to lengthen the loch and to build a dam, although fortunately this did not ruin the lovely scenery. Loch Rannoch, bordered by the Black Wood of Rannoch, is also incorporated in this scheme.

Close by is the historic Pass of Killiecrankie, a densely wooded pass on the banks of the River Garry. One mile south of here was the site of a famous and bloody battle which was fought in 1689 between the Jacobite supporters of James VII, led by Viscount Dundee (immortalised in Walter Scott's ballad *Bonnie Dundee*), and the army of William III, under General Mackay. The Jacobites won the battle, but Viscount Dundee was killed at the very moment of victory. A stone marks the spot where he fell. In the centre of the pass is the romantically named Soldier's Leap, where it is said that a trooper from Mackay's force jumped right across the river to escape from his pursuers. Today the pass is a noted beauty spot and it is hard to visualise its tragic history.

Glamis Castle is perhaps the most historic and fascinating building in the region. It is supposed to have been the setting for Shakespeare's great tragedy of *Macbeth* – Macbeth was the Thane of Glamis – although this has never been proved. In reality, Glamis was a royal residence as long ago as the eleventh century, although the existing castle was founded in the fourteenth century and rebuilt in the style of a French château in 1675. The Old Pretender, the son of James VII of Scotland and II of England, stayed here for a short while in 1715.

The castle has been the ancestral home of the Earls of Strathmore since 1372, and Queen Elizabeth the Queen Mother, who is a member of that great family, spent much of her childhood here. Princess Margaret, the sister of H.R.H. Queen Elizabeth II, was born here in the castle in 1930.

The interior of Glamis contains many notable architectural features, including a lovely panelled chapel, a plaster ceiling of 1621 in the drawing room, and some fine collections of armour, paintings, and furniture. The Lion-cup of Glamis, mentioned in Scott's *Waverley*, is preserved within the castle and is one of its greatest treasures.

The castle is reputedly haunted, and there is also a grim legend that somewhere within its walls is concealed a secret room in which a monster lurks. Supposedly, only the Earl and his heir know the nature of this secret.

Surrounding the castle are beautiful grounds bordered by the Dean Water. There is a splendid sundial to be seen, with eighty-four dials.

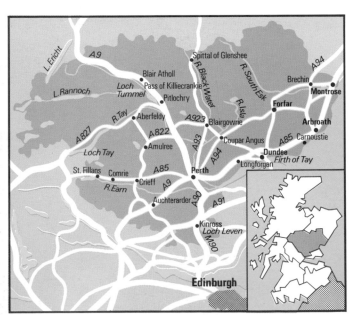

106. *Queen's View, overlooking Loch Tummel.*

108. *Loch Earn is a centre for sailing.*

107. *The River Tummel near the Pass of Killiecrankie.*

109. *The ancient Glamis Castle.*

110. *Loch Rannoch is ten miles long.*

Islands

The Outer Hebrides, also known as the Western Isles, are separated from the Scottish mainland by a stretch of water called the Minch. Because of their remote situation, these islands have largely avoided the spread of urbanisation, and they are one of the last outposts of Gaelic folklore and culture. The Gaelic language is still spoken here. In the eleventh century the Norsemen settled here but the islands were regained by Scotland after the Norsemen were defeated at the battle of Largs, in 1263.

The chain of islands making up the Outer Hebrides is 130 miles in length and the landscape throughout is unspoilt. The coastal scenery has, over the centuries, been eroded into dramatic contours by the full force of the Atlantic Ocean; there are also moorlands and hill country, mile upon mile of sandy beaches and a scattering of crofts and fishing villages. The most important industry is the weaving of Harris tweed.

The largest town of the Outer Hebrides is Stornoway, Isle of Lewis, which has grown up around its fine natural harbour where herring fishing is a thriving occupation. Lewis is actually connected to Harris (between them they extend for more than sixty miles) but the boundary between the two is marked by the mountain of Clisham. At 2,622 feet, Clisham is the highest peak in the Hebrides.

Most important of the other islands in the group are the infertile but lovely Barra, South Uist with its many associations with Bonnie Prince Charlie, and North Uist which has prehistoric standing stones and stone circles. Between North and South Uist is the tiny island of Benbecula, covered by a maze of little lochs.

A second group of islands, the Orkneys, are situated about twenty miles off the northernmost point of the Scottish mainland. The first colonisers were probably the Picts, and Norsemen occupied the islands for about 500 years. They were annexed to Scotland in 1468. The Orkney scenery is fabulous, the climate is mild and, due to the geographical position of the islands, the nights here do not grow dark during the summertime.

Altogether, there are about seventy islands in the group but only twenty-eight are inhabited. By far the largest is Mainland, and here are the two most important towns, Stromness and Kirkwall. At Kirkwall is the famous St Magnus Cathedral, founded in 1137 by Earl Rognvald, the Norse ruler of Orkney, in memory of his murdered predecessor, Magnus. The cathedral was desecrated by Cromwell's army, and in 1671 the spire was destroyed by lightning but the building has now been repaired.

Although all the Orkneys have beautiful scenery, the most spectacular is found on the island of Hoy, which is the second largest of the group. Ward Hill on Hoy is the highest point of the Orkneys, at 1,165 feet, and many rare plants grow on its slopes, but it is the cliff scenery that is the most impressive feature of the island. To the north-west, these cliffs soar above the sea for over 1,000 feet, and actually rising out of the sea is the huge, isolated rock stack known as the Old Man of Hoy. This is 450 feet high and was first climbed in 1966. Further south is Berry Head, where the cliffs are strangely but beautifully coloured.

Hoy is Britain's most southerly breeding place for that rare bird, the Great Skua.

111. *Stornoway harbour and Lewis Castle, Isle of Lewis.*

113. *Marwick Head and the Kitchener Monument on Mainland, Orkney.*

115. *This croft stan— Loch Bee on the isla— South—*

114. *The herring fishing port of Castlebay, on the Isle of Barra.*

116. *The circle of star— stones at Callanish,— L—*

Index

ISBN (*Limp*) 0–7117–0109–1
ISBN (*Cased*) 85306 846 1

© 1985 Jarrold and Sons Ltd, Norwich, England. Published and printed in Great Britain by Jarrold and Sons Ltd, Norwich. 385.